When Mr. Wright
Comes in the Wrong Package

When Mr. Wright Comes in the Wrong Package

Love Him from the Inside Out

Sondra J. Wright

BellaHOUSE
PUBLISHING

Greensboro, NC

When Mr. Wright Comes
in the Wrong Package

Copyright 2012 Sondra J. Wright

ISBN 978-0-9831265-1-5

Library of Congress Control Number: 2012921807

Manufactured in the United States of America

BellaHouse Publishing
P. O. Box 36355
Greensboro, NC 27416-6355
www.bellahousepub.com

TABLE OF CONTENTS

DEDICATION

To my beloved husband John,
fifteen years ago, we had this poem printed in
our wedding program. It reflected perfectly my
feelings at that moment, and with the passing
of time, has grown more perfect in its expression
of my heart for you.

"God gave me a great treasure
of immense and untold worth
And brought a touch of heaven
to my lifetime, here on earth
For he sent me something wonderful
an angel from above
When he blessed me with
the gift of you
My friend, my joy, my love."
~Don Guidry

ACKNOWLEDGMENTS

First of all, I want to thank my husband of fifteen years, John, for being the inspiration behind this book. Thank you for seeing, very early, what I could not, and for never giving up on what you knew would be "*us*."

Families don't come any better than mine and I can't thank you all enough, for your consistent and unwavering belief, love and support. And to my mom and dad especially, who in the summer of 2013, will celebrate their 50th wedding anniversary. Thank you for setting the standard.

Loving acknowledgements to my mother-in-law and late father-in-law, who enjoyed sixty-one years of marriage before his passing last year. Thank you for preparing a gentleman for me, and for teaching him, through example and instruction, the principles of being a godly husband.

Juanita Dix, you are the most fun and talented graphic artist and book designer I could ever have the pleasure of knowing. Thanks for another home run my friend!

To *That Literary Lady*, Yolanda M. Johnson-Bryant, thank you for insisting that I "get it done" and allowing neither the flu nor a computer virus to keep you from proof reading, editing, and getting us to publication on time.

Also, to coach Wende Sanders, for loving the idea of this book and lending to it your voice and invaluable, expert, professional insights.

And these acknowledgements could never be complete without expressing my joyful gratitude and sincere praise for the infinite blessings of God; the One who gave us love, the One who is love, and the One whom without, there is no love.

INTRODUCTION

"Soul-mates are people who bring out the best in you. They are not perfect but are always perfect for you."
—Author Unknown

Let me start by saying that I am far from being a relationship expert—at least not in the capacity of being a professional coach or counselor. I don't give singles advice on how to find love, nor do I offer couples advice on how to stay in love.

Let me also add that I am not writing this book because I have the *perfect* husband *or* the *perfect* marriage. In fact, I would suggest running from anyone who presents themselves to you as a relationship "guru", who has a perfect mate, the perfect marriage, who can unlock secrets of the universe and do the same for you, too. The simple truth is, there is no such thing. And I'm here to tell you, remaining in hot pursuit of what does not exist will leave you frustrated, exhausted, and eternally, single—*always*!

What I do bring you is sound and practical wisdom resulting from a lifetime of getting it wrong, resolving to be alone, with myself, and alas, stumbling upon getting it right.

As I celebrate my fifteenth wedding anniversary, I write this book because, in a completely, imperfect state, I have hit the relationship jackpot. I have a deep and profound gratitude for the imperfect mate and imperfect marriage that I have, and an earnest desire for others to know the same perfectly, imperfect bliss.

There are too many of my sister friends who share the common grievance of not being able to find a good man. And, although I am writing from my own experience as a woman, this frustration comes from both sides of the table. Many men also lament that they are unable to find a good woman. The truth is, there are plenty of good men, and women, in this world, you just have to find the one that's good for you. So, to the gentlemen looking for love, don't let the title fool you, because there's as much here for you as there is for the ladies.

To my over forty ladies looking for love, let me caution you against buying into the lies and stereotypes concerning your increasingly waning possibilities for romance and matrimony. Do not give foolishness permission to set up shop in your head. As with all things, your actions will follow your beliefs, and your outcomes will follow your actions. We've all heard things like, "Single women over forty have a better chance of getting struck by lightning—TWICE, than getting married!" If you're looking to self-destruct, then that's exactly what you should believe. However, if you're looking to score a loving relationship, then choose to believe this instead: *You're never too old to find or fall in love.* In fact, age actually works to your advantage here because those thirty-five and older tend to be more serious about finding long term relationships. The age hype is just there to sell you more anti-aging cream. Don't buy it sister girl!

I promise you, we can all have our happily ever after. But first you have to be willing to get out of your own way, toss past hurts and disappointments in the river, drop all preconceived notions about who you think you are, what you think you want, and prepare yourself for when *Mr. or Mrs. Wright* comes to you in the most unlikely package.

Run Girl! Run!

"An intimate relationship does not banish loneliness. Only when we are comfortable with who we are can we truly function independently in a healthy way, can we truly function within a relationship. Two halves do not make a whole when it comes to a healthy relationship: it takes two wholes." –Patricia Frye

Against my mother's strongly expressed wishes, I married at twenty-three. I thought I was in love . . . . mind you, I said thought—or at least enough to be married. She thought I was "insane." But, as it is with many mother-daughter relationships, I thought I knew best.

I ended up in the middle of a Justice of the Peace ceremony, in which my parents did not attend. On the way to the courthouse, I remember my, *ahem*, perfect mate stopping for fuel. As I sat in the car . . . waiting, I could hear my inner voice screaming for me to jump out of the car, run as fast as my legs would carry me and not look back.

Run girl, run! Jump out of the car and run!

1

I placed my hand on the door handle, looked up the street, and then down, in frantic search of which way to go. For a brief moment, I had forgotten my brother and his roommate, Tim, were riding in the backseat, until I heard Tim's voice ask, "Gee, are you okay?" The sound of his voice piercing through the quiet had shaken me back to my reality. I turned up the car radio, tuned the voices out, and settled back into my seat.

The ceremony was scheduled for 10:00 a.m.—we were back home by 11:00 a.m. Sick to my stomach, I crawled in bed and slept until the next morning.

I had always said that I would get married at twenty-three, and he would be tall, dark, and handsome. Well, here I was, twenty-three, he was tall, dark, and met my criteria for handsome. He was a nice package on the outside, just not a lot to offer on the inside.

Certain the marriage would be short lived, my mother checked in with me frequently and never ended a conversation without asking, "Did you remember to take your birth control pill?" Some days she would ask me to take another one, just to be sure.

Thirty-three months later, at the age of twenty-six, I was divorced. I can only sum the marriage up as an experience that would steal my innocence and forever change the way I viewed men, love and relationships. But I never play the blame game or the victim. We all have to take responsibility for the roles we play in our own conditions and circumstances. Sure, it makes us feel good to have someone to condemn, someone to point the finger at, or someone that we can, at the very least, describe to our girlfriends as the *"low-down-dirty-dog"*—the one that did this, that and the other to us.

The truth is, we're not relationship submissive—we don't live in a country where our mates are selected for us. We are not purchased by the highest bidder or ordered from a catalog. We're all active participants who make conscious decisions about the love and lovers we want in our lives. And if we're willing to dissect relationships honestly, we'll expose the truth and admit the parts we played in our own demise. When you're willing to see it and own it, you're much less likely to repeat it.

A Pig in
a Mud Hole

"People - not just in their teenage years - hold on to this fantasy of love when they're not ready to have a real relationship." —Keri Russell

No sooner than my marriage ended, another relationship was beginning. It was safe, it was healing, and it lasted two years longer than my marriage had. We got along well. We had similar interests, lots of fun, minimal disputes, I loved his family, his family loved me, and we became engaged. He was a great guy, but something in me knew he would not have been a good husband—for someone else, perhaps, just not the right one for me. I won't waste your time explaining what made him the wrong guy, as this book is not intended to address identifying Mr. Wrong. Anyway, chances are, many of you who'll be reading this have already had ample experience in that department.

I remember it well because it was the day our wedding invitations were supposed to go in the mail, and I was feeling very uneasy. Those voices started asking me questions again.

Are we doing the right thing? Are we in love enough to be married or are we marrying because we feel it's the natural progression of things? Is this really what we want or is it what we feel we "should" be doing—the next practical step in a four-year relationship where we were already cohabitating—for three?

I had to wonder if we were getting married because we were two people that shared a deep and mutual love and respect for each other. Did we bring out the best in each other? Did we long to protect and take care of each other? Were we willing to put the needs of the other before our own? Were we ready to live out the rest of our lives, the good, the bad—and everything in between, with each other?

I was certain I was not marrying him for fear of being alone, because one thing I knew for sure, was that a marriage could be the loneliest place on earth. But I couldn't ignore the overwhelming feeling that something was wrong, nor the fact that when these doubts screamed in my ears, urging me to take action and cancel marriage number one, I didn't listen. And, by not listening, I had paid dearly.

So, I did the only thing any reasonable person, with my history, in a state of pre-wedding panic could do.

I uttered those words that many woman have felt, but lacked the courage to speak. "You know, I was thinking that maybe we should postpone the wedding for a while."

And, do you know, this joker agreed? Without an ounce of hesitation or a pound of reservation, he jumped on that suggestion like a pig in a mud hole and I was mortified! I mean, we were literally about to take our wedding invitations to the post office! If he had felt that way, what the heck had he been waiting for? Would he have gone through the motions and left me standing at the altar? Would he have shown up at the altar, gotten married and been a miserable, emotionally distant jerk afterwards?

Anyway, who cared? I had what I needed. Past experiences had left an indelible mark on my brain and I knew to run, not walk, to the nearest exit. I packed my stuff, moved out and never looked back.

Painful? You better believe it! There had been no huge fight, no opportunity to fall out of love, no chance for feelings to fade; just a brave decision to run like hell. And I will be eternally grateful to my girl, Tracy German-Jones, who took her last vacation day from work, to help me pull myself out of a mini, post break-up melt down. Here's to the girlfriends, the really good ones, who always have our backs!

My Latest,
My Greatest Inspiration

"Don't rush into any kind of relationship. Work on yourself. Feel yourself, experience yourself and love yourself. Do this first and you will soon attract that special loving other." —Russ Von Hoelscher

I have heard many women say they manifested their mates by describing what they wanted down to the tiniest detail.

They'd spent time, everyday, envisioning Mr. Right and their wedding day, or focusing on magazine cutouts of happy couples and weddings that had been placed on their vision board.

While I do believe in the power of visualization, especially in combination with some actual work, I did not employ this strategy in my love life. I had actually decided that what we want, or at least what we think we want—because in reality we often don't know—is not always best for our lives.

I've heard it said that because God has a sense of humor, He will often give us what we ask for and sit back and laugh at the mess. But, when it's all said and done, He loves us enough to help us pick up those broken shattered pieces, start anew, and create something beautiful from the mess.

Well, this time I decided not to give God a laugh at my expense, and to leave the selection process entirely up to Him. I felt that if it went wrong, it wouldn't be my fault . . . it would be His. My only request was that whoever the man was, he could lead me spiritually, not the other way around.

After that, I closed the book on love and started exploring life, for the very first time, as a single woman.

Something strange happens when you shut the door on romance. Men start coming out of every nook and cranny, and crawling from underneath every rock and out of every hole imaginable. Lack of interest must emit a powerful pheromone because it seems as if overnight I became a man magnet, and a long list of assorted characters began checking me out as if I was the last hot wing at a tailgate party.

When the phone rang at 3:00 a.m., it startled me. My drowsy "Hello," connected with the melodic voice of Teddy Pendergrass playing in the background:

I've been so many places, I've seen so many things
But none quite so lovely as you
More beautiful than the Mona Lisa

Worth more than gold
And my eyes have the pleasure to behold

You're my latest and my greatest . . .

You're My Latest, My Greatest Inspiration played, and a familiar voice on the other end joined in the chorus and, afterwards, professed his love, declared his commitment and asked me to be his wife.

We had met a couple months earlier when I had taken my car to be serviced. He was a single dad raising a beautiful, young, doe eyed daughter who had stolen my heart. While I had made it very clear to him that I had no interest in dating, I had also made the mistake of allowing myself to get attached to her, and she to me. I had spent too much time with them at the bowling alley, the skating rink and the movies. Signals had gotten mixed up, and now, I felt extremely sad that this man had wasted such a beautiful proposal on a woman who didn't feel the same about him.

It was about eighteen months into my dating sabbatical and I was really enjoying being single. I was travelling and for the first time, really getting to know who I was. Since my very first boyfriend in 8th grade, there had always been a guy in my life. Not a lot of guys, because my relationships always seemed to have longevity, but historically when one had ended, another soon began. Now this time was all about discovering myself. I was growing mentally, emotionally and spiritually, and my self-esteem was reaping the benefits. I felt confident, powerful and happy. And it felt so good finding, falling in love, and just being with . . . *me*. In my newfound bliss, I was completely oblivious to the still, quiet force working behind the scenes, a force that had begun to carefully orchestrate a series of events that would shift the tides and reset my course. Yep, a storm of life-changing proportions was brewing, and yours truly was right in the eye of it.

Cordially Invited

"Every person, all the events of your life are there because you have drawn them there. What you choose to do with them is up to you." —Richard Bach

You are cordially invited to the wedding ceremony of
Elizabeth "Marie" Marshall
and
James "Pete" Pinnix

It was a beautiful Saturday in August and a perfect day for a wedding. *Marie* had been a beloved coworker and dear friend, and we were all excited to share in the joy of her day.

Outside of the church had become a buzzing meeting ground, where current and past coworkers gathered after the ceremony to "*ooh*" over the bride, "*aah*" over the groom, reminisce, and catch up. I hadn't seen my friend Jim since he'd left American Express and relocated to Virginia. We exchanged a friendly hug and a couple rounds of "*long time, no see*" and "*you really look good.*" He introduced me to a couple of guys that were with him, and, after that, I left the church grounds and headed to the reception.

The Keys to Your New Home

"If he won't at least mow your lawn, don't let him come anywhere near your house." —Scott Guthrie, Realtor

It happened so fast that it made my head spin. I had heard all the horror stories about purchasing a home—chasing paperwork, lost documents and closing delays. For me, the experience had been as smooth as churned butter. The loan officer even told me it had been one of the easiest applications he had ever processed, which he attributed to me being so organized with my paperwork. Score one for the *Type A's!*

My realtor had been wonderful—a white haired, mild mannered gentleman, whom I could tell didn't take me seriously at first, but that was okay. Within a few short days of our meeting, he had completely taken me under his wing, patiently teaching me and guiding me through the process of first-time home ownership.

I'll never forget my closing day, as he walked me to my car, and handed me the keys to my new home. He looked me in the eyes, much like a father would a daughter, and issued these words of wisdom, "Young lady, I haven't worked with many single women. You should be very proud of what you've accomplished here. A lot of men out there look to come into a situation where the work has already been done for them. If he won't *at least* mow your lawn, don't let him come *anywhere near* your house."

I promised him that I wouldn't, and with that piece of assurance, he was gone. Little did Mr. Guthrie know, he had nothing to worry about. I was single and satisfied, with a new home of my own. I was not about to let anyone—lawnmower or not—disrupt the peace and solitude in my life or my house.

Snake!!!

"The best day of your life is the one on which you decide your life is your own. No apologies or excuses. No one to lean on, rely on, or blame. The gift is yours – it is an amazing journey – and you alone are responsible for the quality of it. This is the day your life really begins." —Bob Moawad

I thought I would wet my pants at the sight of my mother running out of the small wooded area in my back yard.

My parents' visit was exciting. I hadn't told them about the house until it was almost time to close. And, on this day, they both beamed with pride as they inspected it inside and out. The overgrown brush in the backyard was being viewed from three very different perspectives. I saw a lush, natural area that gave me privacy from the park and neighboring community. My mom saw a grapevine haven and went in search of her beloved muscadines. And my dad, well, my dad saw a breeding ground for the undesirable, and went in search of anything that may pose a threat. And, as the old saying goes: *Be careful what you look for, you just might find it.*

17

"Snaaaaaaaaake!" came piercing through the quiet like an air raid siren, and my four-foot-ten-inch, ninety-five pound mother came sprinting out of those woods at a speed that would have easily qualified her for an Olympic Marathon. Since I'd yet to purchase any yard tools, my dad borrowed a hoe from my neighbor and, you know, did that thing that dads do. It was agreed by all that the lush, natural, grapevine, breeding ground would have to be cleared—at least to a degree that would make it less desirable for snakes and rodents.

The Greatest Homecoming on Earth

"Usually the woman has an appointment with destiny, and the man just happens to be there." —Robert Brault

Nothing fills the city of Greensboro with as much energy, excitement, and fanfare as a North Carolina A&T State University Homecoming. It was October, that special time of year when thousands of alumni, supporters and friends came from near and far to enjoy a variety of activities, festivities and events, all in the spirit of Aggie Pride—*The Greatest Homecoming on Earth*, and this October was no different.

Now, try to remember Jim, whom I mentioned a few pages back. Well, he and I had exchanged phone numbers at the wedding back in August, and had kept in touch. He had always been a laid-back guy—a fun and a well liked supervisor when we all worked together. As I was loading the car for my weekly visit to the laundromat—no washer or dryer yet—he was pulling into the driveway, keeping his promise to check out my place while he was in town for homecoming. We were standing in the back yard and he got a kick out of the snake story and agreed that thinning the brush out was a "*must do*" project.

He asked if I remembered meeting his buddy John whom he had introduced me to at Marie's wedding. I shook my head—a slow no, as I had a vague recollection of him introducing me to few people, but couldn't put a name or face to anyone specifically.

Nonetheless, he went on to explain that John was a very good friend of his whom he trusted to look after his properties in the Piedmont, while he was living and working in Virginia. He offered to give him a call and ask him to come over and make a recommendation to improve the wooded area out back.

Our First Dance

"*Everyone deserves to be loved by someone. You are somebody's someone. And although you may not be aware of them, one day, when you least expect it, you'll find them.*"
—Sondra J. Wright

The cool, fall day had brought with it a cold, steady rain. Let me be clear here, it was pouring cats and dogs. I'd heard a vehicle door close, and an inconspicuous peek through the living room window revealed a man heading through my yard. As he continued towards the side, I ran to the kitchen window to keep him in my view. When he headed towards the back, I repositioned myself so that I could maintain a visual with my target from the window in the back door.

Intrigued by the sight of this peculiar looking man in what appeared to be one of those rugged, 'outdoorsy' *Territory Ahead*-like raincoats, I studied, intently, as he surveyed and assessed my yard for several moments . . . seemingly, undisturbed by the hard rain.

As I think back on it now, it was as if we were unwitting dance partners, separated by a wall. I matched his every move, maintaining visual contact as I advanced from window to window, but careful to keep a distance, as not to be seen.

He was on the move again, heading back towards the front of the house. Wait! Was he approaching the front porch? Why was he coming to my door? Every step he took towards it, I matched with a step away from it—heart pounding with every stride. It was like a scene straight out of a late night horror movie. Then I heard something. It wasn't a knock and it hadn't been the bell. It was more like a faint scratch. Then it stopped, and I heard him walking away. The dance sequence changed. In reverse order, the farther he moved away from the door, the nearer I moved towards it. I heard his truck door shut, I heard the engine start, and then, I heard him drive away. Our first dance had come to an end.

When I was certain he was gone, I opened the door and retrieved the business card he'd left in the doorjamb, announcing the visit of one *John W. Wright, Jr.*

Matchmaker, Matchmaker, Make Me a Match

"Without a single thought, two hands collide and the world finally makes sense again." —Kayla Dawn

I had received several estimates for the clearing project in my backyard, but John's was the lowest. Plus, being a friend of a friend, made me more comfortable about him being at my home.

John was, hands down, one of the nicest guys I had ever met. He was always respectful, had an easy demeanor, was easy to talk with, and he was pleasant to work with. We had similar goals values and beliefs, we had shared some similar life experiences, and a genuine friendship was developing.

Now, playing "Matchmaker" was never my thing because it can be a very risky game. If the match is a success and two people fall madly in love, you get to buy a hideous bridesmaids dress, and give a nice, gushy toast at the reception. Conversely, if the connection is a disaster, you, as cupid, could end up running from your own arrows. So, I had always been wise enough to stay clear of matters pertaining to other people's hearts. But I had an unshakeable instinct about this man—a gut feeling I couldn't ignore and I found myself coming away from every conversation that I'd had with John with one thought in mind: *This is a nice guy who deserves to meet a nice woman. Who can I fix him up with?* I found myself scouring my address book—I *just* had to match my great friend with a great girl.

Too Much Baggage In Memphis

"Sometimes the very thing you're looking for is the one thing you can't see." —Vanessa Williams, *Save the Best For Last*

One of my absolute favorite times of the year was my annual trip to Memphis to visit my sister friend, Brenda. It had become our yearly tradition and with all that had transpired over the past few months, I could certainly use the girl time.

The first night was always spent lying across Brenda's bed, catching up and giggling like teens. And the presence of her new husband Keith had certainly not hampered the experience. In fact, he seemed excited for our reunion. When Keith appeared at the bedroom door to hand me the phone, I was a little confused at first. *Who would be calling me here?*

When John had asked for a telephone number where he could reach me—just in case he needed to, I never imagined he would use it—and certainly not to make sure I had arrived safely. But, indeed he had. And this made my girlfriend Brenda wide-eyed and giddy with questions. She was newly remarried to a really great man, and had been on me about dating again. I had avoided the conversation so far, but John's call had given her just the right opportunity *and* ammunition to broach the subject.

"Who's that? He sounds really nice, Sondra! What about him?" And I remember lying across the bed wrinkling my nose incredulously at her suggestion that he may be "*the one.*"

"Girl no! He's got too much baggage!"

Yes, John was easy to talk to, and we'd had many open and relaxed conversations—not all about the business of my yard. He was a nice guy, no doubt, but he was going through, shall I say, a period of transition, and my disinterest in dating had not been altered in meeting him. We were becoming friends, and that was all. I didn't see him in *that* way, never regarded him as anything more— that was the end of that.

A Rose By Any Other Name

"I came here tonight because when you realize you want to spend the rest of your life with somebody, you want the rest of your life to start as soon as possible." —Billy Crystal as Harry Burns, *When Harry Met Sally*

Memphis was a blast, as always, but there was no place like home. I arrived home during the early evening, unpacked, did laundry, and settled in to read the mail. Amongst the magazines, bills and credit card offers, was a blue envelope with a card inside that read:

What's a nice person like you, doing so far away, from a nice person like me?

The bottom was signed:

Welcome Home, John.

Aww, that's nice, I thought and tossed it on the sofa table.

It wasn't long after I went to bed that the phone rang. It was Jim calling to catch up, and several minutes into our chat, my call waiting signaled that I had another caller.

How had I missed it? Was I so turned off to men, love, romance, relationships, and dating that I had completely missed every clue, every hint, every signal that John was into me? He phoned me every day. We hung out at Lowe's and Home Depot a couple days a week, often for hours at the time. He had called to check on me when I was in Memphis. He'd even left a sappy card in my mailbox. Now, he was on the phone, not the usual light and happy John that I was used to, but a little more serious this time.

I listened quietly as he shared how his feelings for me had grown over the past several weeks, how much he looked forward to any amount of time we spent together, how much he had missed me while I was away, and how much he'd like our relationship to be more than it currently was.

"I'd like to take you out," he said.

And without a moment's hesitation, my response was a solid, "No."

"Why not?"

"Because you're married John, that's why not!"

Yep, my boy John had himself a wife. And not only a wife, but two children came along with that baggage. I knew the back-story. They had been separated for a while and not for the first time. I had tried to convince him to put the marriage back together, especially for the sake of the children, and he had explained that it wasn't possible—the marriage was irreparably broken.

His response sounded frustrated. "I'm not married, I'm separated!"

"Still married," I replied.

"But you know my situation."

"Yes. And I really don't want anything to do with it."

"Well, if you don't want to go out, maybe I could bring a movie over sometime, and some dinner, or maybe we could order in?"

"John, I don't care what you call it. A rose by any other name still has thorns and I will not date a married man!"

He was immediately apologetic and moved in for damage control. I thought it was nice of him to want to make sure the friendship was still intact and he was satisfied to go on in the manner in which we had been—great conversations and hanging out at local home improvement stores. And that was fine with me because I had nothing more to give. If the marriage was over then yes, he deserved to move forward in life with someone, but not me. Even if I were open and available, I found the idea of a potentially difficult ex-wife, two children, financial obligations, and all the other uncertainties of dating a divorced man, to be a tad bit overwhelming and certainly not anything I had pictured on the story board of my life. Others had done it successfully, yes, but it was not the right package for me. No thanks!

Beware the Promises of Men

"Meeting you was fate, becoming your friend was a choice, but falling in love with you I had no control over."
—Unknown

The end of another year was fast approaching. John had delayed the clearing work in my backyard until late fall, after all the leaves had dropped.

It was mid-December, the project was coming to an end, and the back yard really looked nice. He had a stone mailbox built, planted a beautiful Japanese Maple, and added some other really nice touches to enhance the front lawn. I was more than pleased. Mr. Guthrie, my realtor, would have been too.

In addition to Lowes and Home Depot, we both enjoyed scouting furniture stores and antique shops. I tried to drive my car most of the time because riding in his early model pickup truck was an adventure in and of itself. Smiling and pretending not to smell the fumes was one thing, but trying to ignore the fact that I could see clear down to the street through the hole in the floorboard beneath my feet, was something altogether different. And, Lord help me because it was cold and I could see my pure breath when I talked. It was a heatless box of faded red metal disguised as an old Chevy truck, but he was so cool about it. He sat tall, straight and proud behind the wheel, handling "*Big Red*" (that's what he called her) like she was a Phantom Rolls Royce.

I had no idea his birthday was on New Year's day, but he didn't hesitate to let it be known. With the day fast approaching, he pleaded his case about not having been out in a while and just really wanting to enjoy a nice dinner and a movie in celebration of his birthday.

"I *promise* Sondra, it's not a date. Just dinner and a movie for my birthday, that's all!"

And *so* . . . I agreed.

Our non-date date turned out to be the best New Year's Eve of my life. Dinner conversation flowed easily and effortlessly, and at some point in the evening, I became aware of the approving smiles and gazes from the people seated around us. After the movie, we paid a visit to my girlfriend, Tony, who liked him immediately. I spent the entire visit rolling my eyes at her and trying to ignore the hilarious facial expressions of admiration and thumbs up gestures she made when he wasn't looking.

Upon leaving her house, she grabbed me and whispered in my ear, "You stop being mean to him Gee. I like him, he's sweet."

After that night, we were inseparable. That new year was a turning point. With it, came the easiest and most comfortable relationship of my life. I had been blessed with a really great guy—my glass slipper, my perfect fit. And, when I decided to relax and allow him to love me, the ex-wife, children, and old truck with deadly fumes no longer seemed to matter.

The blinding fog of limitation had lifted from my mind, revealing a man who was hard-working, disciplined and always reliable. I saw that he was smart and talented. He was considerate, supportive, and respected by his peers. I appreciated his constant reassurance and the patience he showed me as I faced many moments of uncertainty. I loved the love that he had for his family, especially his children, and knew how very lucky I would be to experience just a portion of that.

Being with him brought back a fond memory of my parents. My dad would sometimes chase my mom through the kitchen with one of those fat, red sausages. He'd catch her, of course, then smack her on the butt as she giggled, "Stop!" I'd pretend to be disgusted because I was a teenager and that's what teenagers are supposed to do. But through the fake repulsion, I was watching, I was learning, and I knew one day, I'd have a man who'd chase me, smack me, and make me laugh out loud. I had fallen in love with *Mr. Wright* from the inside out, and I was wonderfully content. And, deep inside, I knew I had found the one—the one who'd chase me with his sausage, smack me on the butt, and make me giggle, "Stop!"

The following year, we were married.

Peanut Butter and Bananas? Yuck!

"Any relationship primarily built on physical attractiveness is predestined to be short lived."—Zig Ziglar

One Christmas evening, while at my in-laws, our family got into a lively discussion about some of our favorite odd food combinations—Wendy's French fries dipped in chocolate Frosty, potato chips and hot sauce, cashews wrapped in honey wheat bread, and pickles sprinkled with grape Kool-Aid. The list of combinations were endless and as unique and wacky as we were. It's funny how the recipes we find so yummy can sound so unappealing to others.

Of all the unusual pairings shared that evening, it was my brother-in-law's passion for peanut butter and banana sandwiches that I considered most unlikeable. I love to eat peanut butter every day, right off the spoon. I also enjoy bananas, in a sandwich, cereal, or simply by itself. But, the two together, I just could not imagine.

"*Hey sis,*" he said, "*don't knock it 'til you've tried it!*" And so, I did.

It was several days after Christmas, and I was completely burned out on holiday leftovers. My stomach was signaling that it was time to eat, and while my taste buds were very clear on what they didn't want, they provided not a clue on what they *did* want.

Eyeing the banana on the counter I thought a banana sandwich with a little Miracle Whip just might do the trick. But, in that moment, remembering the tantalizing description of my brother-in-law's favorite combination, my curiosity got the best of me. I grabbed the creamy Jif® peanut butter, a staple, from the cabinet. Literally, not wanting to bite off more than I could chew, I peeled the banana back gingerly, put just a smidgen of peanut butter on the tip, went in for a bite and couldn't help but smile at the unbelievable flavor sensation being experienced by my mouth. How could I, at this age, not have known the simple pleasure of peanut butter and banana?

Often we're so rigid about our likes and dislikes, or what we think we like and dislike, that we refuse to take a chance on something new. Inevitably, the consequence is that we miss out on an entire world of great things, great foods, great jobs, and potentially great partners.

Recently, on my Facebook timeline, I ran across a post from Mia, a thirty-something friend, that asked:

"Ladies, would you date someone your height or shorter than you?"

Here is the conversation thread that followed. The identities, except for mine, have been changed to protect the innocent—and the guilty.

Terra – Not shorter, I'm 5'2 LOL.

Mia – Wow! Yeah you can't go shorter LOL.

Kris – Nope!

Mia – Seems like there's a shortage of men with good height these days; LOL. I'm sorry if I'm picky, but sometimes I see nice looking men but they are midgets. LOL

Terra – I'm dating one; LOL

Mia – You're dating one shorter than you?

Terra – He's a nice looking man but he is a midget.

Kris – Date a treasure troll? no no no!

Meshia – Me either, not shorter . . .

Reva – I'm 5'4! HELL NO! You can NOT get along with a short man. He is always right, knows everything, and they ALWAYS have something to prove!

Terra – OMG so true Reva! You guys are cracking me up!

Mia – I'm 5"4 also, and you are right, the shorter guys are cocky. I guess a lot of people take advantage of them.

Reva – I like them big, tall, and BLACK as 4 o'clock in the morning!

Sondra – Mia, don't toss a potential life mate because he's a little shorter. How does the man treat you? How does he make you feel? Do you want similar things in life? Is he supportive, caring, kind, compassionate, respectful, goal oriented, and God fearing. Does he have all his teeth? Why don't you give a man an inch for each of his positive traits, and see how tall he looks to you then!

Terra – So true Sondra.

Mia – True but if he is shorter than me I don't want to carry him. I know it sounds petty but I think it would really bother me. Now watch a guy comes on here and comments that size don't matter; LOL

Reva – Sondra I realize that I, as a plus size woman, am NOT every man's preference so I HOPE that it is OK if EVERY MAN is NOT mine. I just can NOT take a man who is shorter than me seriously!

Terra – And its ok to have preferences. It's better to know what you want.

Sondra – Reva, Terra, absolutely it's okay to have preferences. But just because you preference something doesn't mean you wouldn't appreciate something else – if you tried it.

Meisha – Yes, but people think that you're "judging" an individual because you don't preference them. That's not true.

Terra – You're right. I don't judge, that's why I have a short man.

Sondra – I'm simply suggesting that it may not be wise to be bound by your preferences. There are lots of women who claim they can't find a good man. But a good man can be hard to see if you're looking at him through rose colored glasses. We've all witnessed it – model type women, strolling through the mall, smiling, cuddling and holding hands with a short, round, or some other type man that's not on our "preference" list, and wondered to yourself or aloud "How in the world did he end up with her?!" I promise, you…that woman is as happy as she can be. Get over yourself, get out your way, and let a good man come into your life; SHORT, BALD and ALL!!

Terra – Well said

Mia - Sondra I think it's a difference of preference and being too picky, looks is not everything but it does matter, and if people say it doesn't, they are lying to themselves. If I'm not attracted, it's not going to work. Someone out there may not think I'm attractive, that's fine, they are not meant for me. That's why everyone has different taste and preferences. It's not everything but you must have that attraction. That's why people cheat.

Sondra – I hear you Mia. I just don't want your preferences to get in the way of happiness, that's all. Believe me, I get the whole "chemistry" thing between two people but shallow breathing, sweaty palms, and an elevated heart rate can also cause you to overlook warning signs of potential problems down the road. And listen, cheaters come up with a myriad of excuses for having affairs but it has more to do with the cheaters selfishness than with their partners looks, height, size, style or any of that superficial stuff. Remember that.

Meisha – I get what you're saying Mia. Sometimes people grow on you though, especially if they take time to build a friendship instead of wanting to jump right into a relationship.

Mia – I don't think I'm picky to the point where he has to be exactly 6ft tall, but I was just wondering what ladies thought about actually date someone 5' or 5'2 if they were 5'5 or 5'6.

Kimmy – Yes I'm doing it now. I'm 5'4 and he is 1 inch taller than me, so in a good shoe honey, it's over!! It is a first but the blessing came in a package I never expected. He is the perfect man for me. What he is missing in height he truly makes up for in character, integrity and his love for me and my children.

Mia – 1 inch is not that bad Kimmy. What if he were way shorter?

Kimmy – I think I would still do it. I've learned that good things come in the least likely package. I was always attracted to taller, darker than dirt brothers, but I now have the total opposite of that and I'm so content.

Mia – Wow. That's great!

And, height is just the beginning of a list of the reasons women deem a potentially great partner un-datable, before even giving him a chance to show what real qualities he may have to offer.

While some see shy men as a curse, I see the shy man as a blessing. You say he's so shy he won't approach you? Good! That means if you're dating him, there is a great probability that he won't approach another woman either!

Is he jobless? Listen, being underemployed or unemployed is not the same as being unmotivated. And, especially in today's economic climate, overlooking this guy is something you'll want to consider very carefully. If your standards are compatible and you see potential and drive, work with him. You just may have a future executive or successful entrepreneur in your sights.

Men with body features that standout, like big butts and man boobs, certainly find themselves on the list of un-datables. But listen, if he's packing an apple bottom or a cup size that's bigger than yours, the upside is you can probably feel completely comfortable strutting around the house butt naked without being judged.

And, what is it about that "*momma's boy*" that makes a girl want to run for the hills? I always heard that if you want a good idea of how a man is going to treat you, take note of how he treats his momma.

How about the ones with no swag, no game, or just too nice? You're either single or keep dating the wrong guys because your priorities are all off. What's swag got to do with it? Absolutely nothing! And, eighteen months from now, when you pass his too nice, swag-less behind in the mall, content as a baby lamb with his pregnant wife on his arm, just proceed to the nearest ladies room and kick yourself in the head.

How many good men have you possibly dismissed? Perhaps it's time to reevaluate your "*preferences.*" Your shallow dating pool will get a little deeper when you re-fuse to let age, distance, or lack of fashion forwardness stop you from finding your happily ever after. It's like Kimmy said, "*Sometimes good things, come in the least likely package.*"

Some Sage Advice

"When nobody around you seems to measure up, it's time to check your yardstick." —Bill Lemley

According to Wende Sanders, Certified Life Coach, Author, and founder of *The Phenomenal Lifestyle*™ *Women's Center*, "By the time we reach adulthood, and have officially become *"grown and sexy,"* we've likely faced numerous disappointments and hurts, especially when it comes to relationships and romance. The desire to protect ourselves from future pain often becomes an obsession for single women, causing them to respond in interesting ways. Many will create a *"list"* of standards so long and detailed, it pretty much dares a man to meet its criteria."

I've witnessed firsthand, fun, attractive, interesting women who set standards that only God himself can meet, and they spend their single days bewildered that they can't find anyone.

Wende uses a housing analogy and says if your true desire is to be in a loving, passionate, and healthy relationship, then focus more on the "*foundation*" and less on the "*finishes.*"

"Building a truly rewarding and lifelong partnership starts much deeper than height, weight or job title. It doesn't mean we should "*settle*" for people who don't stimulate us physically, mentally or emotionally, but it does mean that women—and men—must learn what realistic guidelines look like, and not be completely uncompromising in their standard," says the Life Coach.

In other words, don't set yourself up for failure by creating an unrealistic and unattainable list of expectations. And, give yourself permission, in certain situations, to relax your criteria a bit. Countless men and women have found their *Mr. or Mrs. Wright* looking beyond the superficial.

Ms. Sanders advises women to segment their "*Ideal Man*" list into three categories: *Negotiable, Non-Negotiable,* and *Preference*s. "This allows you to identify everything you want in a partner, but also leaves room for what the Creator knows is best for you."

She also says, "It's essential to have this segmented list before you begin considering a mate. If you wait until after you've met someone you like, you're more likely to begin shaping your list around that specific man. For example, things that would have been non-negotiable for you, like no more than one baby's mama or a non-smoker, all of a sudden become negotiable. This takes a woman from being open and flexible, down the path of compromising her values and her authentic needs."

"Is it nice to have a man that is six-foot-two, with an athletic build and Obama-like swagger? Heck yeah! Is it better to have a husband that's attentive, faithful, and romantic, who makes you laugh and helps around the house? You're darn right it's better! A lot better! The great thing is that there are more men in the second category, than in the first. But, you'll only see them if you open your heart, as well as your mind."

"Your task is not to seek for Love, but merely to seek and find all the barriers within yourself that you have built against it."
——Rumi, thirteenth century Sufi poet

Beautifully, Imperfectly Perfect

"Well, it seems to me that the best relationships - the ones that last - are frequently the ones that are rooted in friendship. You know, one day you look at the person and you see something more than you did the night before. Like a switch has been flicked somewhere. And the person who was just a friend is... suddenly the only person you can ever imagine yourself with." —Gillian Anderson

I'm remembering a cake my mom baked once. The layers were very disagreeable. One side had baked higher than the other, the middle had a sink-hole, and some of the edges had broken off. Though futile, she did her best to fill in the gaping holes and stack the layers in a way that would make the cake appear even. As she started to smooth on her homemade chocolate buttercream frosting, it tore the top layer of the cake, mixing crumbs all throughout. It was one lopsided, lumpy, unsightly piece of confectionary. But when mom was done, she smiled, cut a slice and tasted it. "It might be ugly," she said, "but it sure tastes good!"

In my lifetime, I have seen many attractive cakes that failed to please the palette—wedding and baby shower cakes notoriously, but the cakes considered less outwardly appealing, the ones that would get easily ignored in a bakery window, have never failed to satisfy.

Fifteen years have gone by much too fast. My stepchildren are now grown and starting families of their own. The old Chevy truck is now a fleet of Chevrolet trucks used in the operation of a successful business we've grown together. I can't tell you it was all smooth sailing—conflicts in relationships happen all the time. Disagreements are inevitable. There are times when you, inadvertently, hurt each other's feelings. But, I can tell you one thing it has not been, and that's difficult. The appreciation and respect that we have for each other, as friends and as lovers, runs deep, and I can say, in all earnest, that every twist, turn, up, down and bump in the road, has served to strengthen and solidify us a couple.

I like when we listen to each other like best friends. I like the tenderness that we treat each other with. Most of all, I like the laughter that passes easily between us, like a soothing, comforting breeze that whispers in my ear, *you are safe, you are protected, you are loved.*

There is no one I would rather share the good times, or bad with, no one I would rather share a laugh or a cry with. In its natural, optimal state, what we share is beautifully, imperfectly perfect. Everything I thought was wrong, actually turned out alright.

So here's to you babe, the one I couldn't see myself with, the one I can't see myself without.

And to those who think that love eludes you, here's hoping that you will find the courage to embrace the *least likely package*, only to discover inside, your very own *Mr. or Mrs. Wright.*

Note From the Author

When Mr. Wright Comes in the Wrong Package is about giving yourself permission, to allow a love to come to you from a source you may have never expected—or wrapped in the most *unlikely package*. Renounce the trap of expectation, and free up your perceptions in favor of a love adventure that runs deeper than surface attraction and one that can sustain the tests of time.

The good news is, somewhere inside, you already know this. You feel it in your gut. You know something is wrong with the mate selection strategies you have been using, and, continuing to employ the same plan is only producing more of the same results.

If you're ready to move beyond the cycle of long dates, to a lifelong partnership, dare to make a change. The best matchmakers and relationship coaches know that people need more than a hot and heavy physical connection to function as a successful unit and to be compatible over the long term. Don't settle for tall, dark and handsome with great abs, no kids and a perfect smile. Settle for more. Settle for someone who will make you feel special, who will overlook shortcomings, who will deal with mistakes gently, whose commitment is forever. Be willing to do the same for your mate and you'll be on the path to happily ever after!

About the Author

Sondra J. Wright, a women's empowerment entrepreneur, is passionate about inspiring transformation through self-awareness and innovative thinking. Using her talents as a writer, speaker, and certified behavior specialist, Sondra seeks to make a positive difference by helping women recognize, evaluate, and overcome limiting beliefs, put the squeeze on self-sabotaging behaviors, and attract greater possibilities than they ever thought possible. Visit mrwrightwrongpackage.com